DEVIOUS

Mind-Bending

PUZZLES

**Official
American
Mensa
Puzzle Book**

Terry Stickels

STERLING PUBLISHING CO., INC.
New York

Library of Congress Cataloging-in-Publication Data

2 4 6 8 10 9 7 5 3

Published by Sterling Publishing Co., Inc.
387 Park Avenue South, New York, NY 10016
Portions of this book are extracted
from the following texts, published by
Pomegranate Communications, Inc., California:
Mind-Bending Puzzles 3:
A Storehouse of Stumpers!, © 1999 by Terry Stickels, and
Mind-Bending Puzzles 4:
Provocative Posers, © 1999 by Terry Stickels.
© 2002 by Terry Stickels
Distributed in Canada by Sterling Publishing
$c/_o$ Canadian Manda Group, One Atlantic Avenue, Suite 105
Toronto, Ontario, Canada M6K 3E7
Distributed in Great Britain by Chrysalis Books
64 Brewery Road, London N7 9NT, England
Distributed in Australia by Capricorn Link (Australia) Pty. Ltd.
P.O. Box 704, Windsor, NSW 2756, Australia

Sterling ISBN 0-8069-8077–X

Contents

Introduction

Devious Mind-Bending Puzzles has one sole purpose: for you to have fun. I've designed these brainteasers so they may be solved many different ways. So please don't think there's only one way to solve them. I'll give you the way I solved them in the answer section, but your way may be just as valid.

You'll find word games, math brainteasers, spatial/visual puzzles, and other mind treats, giving you diversity while you stretch your mind and increase your mental flexibility. If you've had a semester of algebra, you'll find it useful in solving some of the puzzles, but don't worry if you haven't...it's not mandatory. I've tried my best to create puzzles for the beginner as well as the advanced puzzle solver.

There's no time limit for any of these puzzles. Take as long as you like or skip to another puzzle and come back later to the one that has you stumped. You'll be amazed how quickly your mind starts piecing things together—and then you'll find the fun I've been discussing.

Good luck and happy puzzling!

—*Terry Stickels*

PUZZLES

1.

Joe takes three-fifths of a bag of candy. Bob has three-fourths of Pete's share of the remaining candy. What fraction of the total number of pieces of candy does Pete have?

2.

What is the value of F in the following system of equations?

$$A + B = Z \quad (1)$$
$$Z + P = T \quad (2)$$
$$T + A = F \quad (3)$$
$$B + P + F = 30 \quad (4)$$
$$A = 8 \quad (5)$$

3.

The following words can all be transformed into new words by prefixing the same three letters, in the same order, at the beginning of the words. What are the three letters?

```
_ _ _  PENT
_ _ _  RATE
_ _ _  VICE
_ _ _  VILE
```

4.

Can you quickly write down the numbers 1 through 5 so that no two consecutive numbers are next to one another? The first number is not 1, and the second, third, and fourth numbers must increase in value.

5.

Arrange the four squares below to create five squares of the same size. You cannot interlock or overlap the squares.

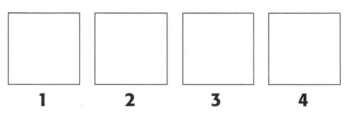

6.

Determine the relationships between the pictures and the letters to find the solutions:

7.

What comes next in this number sequence?
Hint: Get primed for this puzzle.

5   8   26   48   122   ?

8.

Find the hidden phrase or title.

9.

The words *assign* and *stalactite* form a relationship that produces the word *ignite* in parentheses. Can you find a similar relationship between the words *double* and *stationary* that will form a new word in the blank?

assign (ignite) stalactite
double (_____) stationary

10.

What is 1,449 in Roman numerals?

11.

Here's a balance puzzle. Where does the 25-lb. weight on this teeter-totter go (how many feet from the fulcrum)?

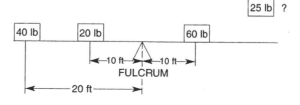

 12.

Find the hidden phrase or title.

 13.

What is $\frac{1}{3}$ divided by $\frac{1}{5}$ divided by $\frac{2}{3}$ times $\frac{3}{5}$?

14.

A group of students at a major university was polled to see which courses they were taking. Sixty-four percent were taking English, 22% were taking a foreign language, and 7% were taking both. What percentage of the students polled were taking neither subject?

15.

You need to match three items, A, B, and C, with three numbers, 1, 2, and 3. But you are given some peculiar information by which to determine how to match them up. From the following rules, can you find a solution?

(a) If A is not 1, then C is not 3.
(b) If B is either 2 or 1, then A is 3.
(c) If C is not 2, then A cannot be 3.
(d) If C is not 1, then A is not 3.
(e) If C is 3, then B is not 1 or 2.
(f) If B is 3, then A is not 2.

16.

Here is a five-letter "trickle-down" puzzle. Change one letter at a time to reach the final word.

TIMER

_____
_____
_____
_____

DUNKS

17.

Find the hidden phrase or title.

18.

Given the initial letters of the missing words, complete this sentence:

There are 6 O in an I.

19.

Quickly now, solve this puzzle! You are taking a long drink of water. Which happens first?

The glass is ⁵/₁₆ empty.
The glass is ⁵/₈ full.

20.

Quickly now, finish this mathematical analogy:

¹/₅ **is to 5 as 5 is to** ___?___ .

21.

Find the hidden phrase or title.

22.

There is a certain logic in the following diagram in the placement of the letters around the triangles. What is the missing letter in the last triangle?

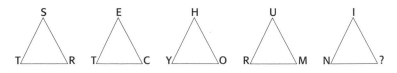

23.

Find the hidden phrase or title.

F R A M E
G A M E

24.

Bill and Tom played several golf matches against each other in a week. They played for a pizza at each match, but no pizzas were purchased until the end of the week. If at any time during the week Tom and Bill had the same number of wins, those pizzas were canceled. Bill won four matches (but no pizzas), and Tom won three pizzas. How many rounds of golf were played?

25.

Judy and Mary are Susan's sister's mother-in-law's son's daughters. What relation is Susan to Judy and Mary?

26.

Find the hidden phrase or title.

27.

One way to make eight 8's equal 100 would be as follows:

$$\frac{8888 - 88}{88} = 100$$

Can you devise at least one other way?

28.

How long will it take for you to find three common, everyday words that contain three straight A's? By straight, I mean that they can be separated by consonants, but not by another vowel.

29.

Find the hidden phrase or title.

30.

What is the missing number in this grid?

12	27	111
19	39	?
4	9	37

31.

A professional bass fisherman caught 30 bass during a five-day tournament. Each day, he caught three more fish than the day before. How many fish did he catch the first day?

32.

Given the initial letters of the missing words, complete this phrase:

86,400 S in a D

Hint: You have up to 24 hours to solve this.

 33.

Fifteen seconds for this one: Unscramble the following letters to come up with a word game everyone knows.

B L A B S C E R

 34.

How many squares are in the figure below?

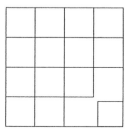

 35.

How many numbers are in the following sequence if all terms are included?

0 3 6 9 12 15 18 ... 960

Here's an alphametic puzzle that isn't too difficult. See if you can replace the letters with the proper numbers to make this puzzle work.

$$
\begin{array}{r}
\text{HE} \\
\times \text{ME} \\
\hline
\text{BE} \\
\text{Y E} \\
\hline
\text{EWE}
\end{array}
$$

37.

Find the hidden phrase or title.

There are two boxers. The smaller boxer is an amateur and also the son of the bigger boxer, who is a professional. But the pro boxer is not the amateur's father. Who is the pro?

39.

Shown below are four ways to divide a four-by-four grid in half. Find the other two ways. No diagonals or rotations allowed (for example, #1 turned 90 degrees doesn't count).

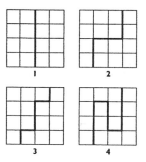

40.

In a game of craps, you are considering betting that the next roll of the dice is going to produce a 2, a 3, or a 12 (not necessarily a come-out roll). A friend who is quick with probabilities advises you against making this bet. Why?

41.

Quickly now, $1/7$ is what percentage of $3/11$?

42.

Seven of the following eight words are related. Which is the odd one out and why?

CALCIUM	**IODINE**
IRON	**MAGNESIUM**
PHOSPHOROUS	**SELENIUM**
TOCOPHEROL	**ZINC**

 43.

Find the hidden phrase or title.

 44.

If two-fifths of a fraction is doubled and then multiplied by the original fraction, the result is $1/15$. What is the original fraction (positive numbers only)?

45.

A palindromic number is one that reads the same forward and backward, such as 8,315,138. There are only three palindromic squares under 1,000. Two of those are $11^2 = 121$ and $22^2 = 484$.

What is the third palindromic square under 1,000?
What is the first palindromic square over 1,000?

46.

A little knowledge of algebra may help here. You've been given $100 and told to buy 100 candles for a party. The first type of candle costs $0.50, the second $5.50, and the third $9.50. You must purchase exactly 100 candles and spend exactly $100. How many candles of each type will you purchase? There is just one solution.

47.

How many triangles are in the figure below?

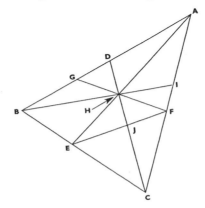

48.

Find the hidden phrase or title.

 49.

What is the next letter in the following sequence?

$$D - N - O - S - A - J - \underline{\ ?\ }$$

Hint: Can time run backward?

 50.

From among the integers 1 through 9, can you find six different integers, call them A, B, C, D, E, and F, such that $A \times B \times C = D \times E \times F$?

Hint: Don't use 5 or 7.

51.

The letters in several words in the English language lend themselves to being recombined into new words. For example, the word *item* can be transformed into *mite*, and *emit*. The letters of the word *vile* can be rearranged to *live*, *evil*, and *veil*. Try to find a four-letter word that can be changed into four new words (five total, counting your original).

52.

A visitor to a zoo asked the zookeeper how many birds and how many beasts were in a certain section of the zoo. The zookeeper replied: "There are 45 heads and 150 feet, and with that information you should be able to tell me how many of each there are." Can you help the visitor?

53.

Complete the following straightforward math sequence puzzle. It is easier than it appears at first glance.

$$240 - 240 - 120 - 40 - 10 - 2 - \underline{\ ?\ }$$

54.

If 28 equals 24 and 68 equals 76, what does 48 equal?

🔨 55.

Following is a word written in a code in which each set of two-digit numbers represents a letter. See if you can decipher the word.

41   51   55   55   32   15   44

Hint 1: Notice that 5 is the highest number used.
Hint 2: Think of rows and columns.

🔨 56.

In the figure, line **AB** is parallel to line **CD**, angle Y = 50°, and angle Z = 140°. How big is angle X?

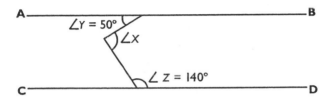

🔨 57.

Determine Figure H in the series below.

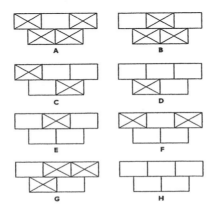

58.

The five words listed here share a common trait. By playing with the letters of each word, see if you can determine the trait.

Hint: The same trait is shared with the words apt, tea, and tar.

rifle — evil — deal — rats — tale

59.

One hundred doctors are attending a medical convention. Each doctor is either a surgeon or a dermatologist. At least one is a dermatologist. Given any two of the doctors, at least one is a surgeon. How many are dermatologists and how many are surgeons?

60.

Given the initial letters of the missing words, complete the following phrase. *Hint:* Think of a musical.

76 T in the B P

61.

Which of the following is larger?

A. $\frac{1}{3}$ times its cube times a dozen cubed
B. $\frac{1}{2}$ times its square times a dozen dozen squared divided by 2 squared times 2 cubed

62.

Here's another alphametic:

After seeing what one round of 18 holes of golf would cost at the new country club, Mary decided that today would be an excellent day to play tennis. How much did the round of golf cost (cart included, of course!)?

S E E S
T E E S
F E E S
C A.S H

 63.

If two gallons of paint are needed to cover all sides of one cube, how many gallons are needed to cover all exposed surfaces of the figure below? Include surfaces on which the figure is resting. Hint: There are no hidden cubes.

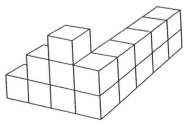

 64.

What is the next number in this sequence?

1 4 9 7 7 9 4 1 9 ?

65.

Find the hidden phrase or title.

 66.

What are the values of R and S?

$$Q + M = C$$
$$C + K = R$$
$$R + Q = S$$
$$M + K + S = 40$$
$$Q = 8$$

 67.

Decipher the following cryptogram.

AGEGLLGO CM BUGAJNL IBD.

68.

Using the number 4 twice and only twice, can you come up with the number 12? You may use any math symbol or sign you wish. Remember, only the number 4 may be used, and only twice.

69.

Complete this wheel:

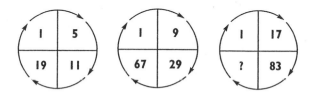

70.

Find the hidden phrase or title.

71.

What is the next figure in the following series?

I ℈ ♉ ⅄ ♈

 72.

One-fifth of a pound of chocolate is balanced perfectly by two-fifths of a block of the same chocolate. What is the weight of the whole block of chocolate?

 73.

Find the hidden phrase or title.

74.

A man played roulette every day and lost money every day. As the story goes, a fortune teller had put a curse on him that he would lose every time he played roulette. For the ten years since, he has been losing consistently every day, yet he is a very wealthy man who has a loving wife and family. In fact, his wife has even accompanied him daily to the roulette table, where he bets either red or black only. How could this family be so wealthy?

75.

You see here a two-dimensional front view and a two-dimensional top view of a three-dimensional object. Can you sketch what the object looks like in three dimensions?

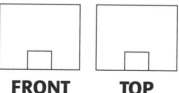

FRONT   TOP

76.

What comes next in this sequence?

$$\frac{1}{1} \quad \frac{9}{8} \quad \frac{5}{4} \quad \frac{4}{3} \quad \frac{3}{2} \quad \frac{5}{3} \quad \frac{15}{8} \quad \frac{?}{}$$

Hint: Think of music.

77.

Find the hidden phrase or title.

78.

Unscramble the following:

TDILUEAT

79.

Six hours ago, it was two hours later than three hours before midnight. What time is it?

The box pictured here has been folded together from one of the four choices given. Which is the correct choice?

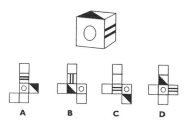

A   B   C   D

81.

What three-letter word can be added to the beginning of these words to form four new words?

RACKS
FLY
RAGE
BELL

82.

A jeweler is offering to cut rare gems into fractions to sell to distributors. For $20 a distributor can purchase $1/40$ of an ounce, or for $40 she can purchase $1/20$ of an ounce. Many of the distributors want another cutting in between these two offerings. An enterprising young dealer opens a store across the street and offers $1/30$ of an ounce for $30. Fair enough, right? Where would you buy your gems, or does it even make a difference?

83.

Find the hidden phrase or title.

 84.

What is the largest sum of money you can have in coins and not be able to make change for a dollar?

 85.

Fill in the blank:

Amelia is the daughter of Amanda. Amanda is the _____ of Amelia's mother.

86.

Find the hidden phrase or title.

87.

If satellite *y* takes three years to make one revolution and satellite *x* takes five years to make one revolution, in how many years will they both be exactly in line as they are now?

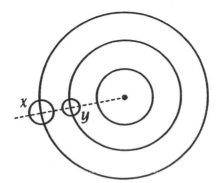

88.

Here is a sequence puzzle consisting of the numbers 0 through 9. Complete the sequence by filling in the remaining numbers. How is the pattern formed?

3   6   9   2   5   8   1   4   ?   ?

89.

Find the hidden phrase or title.

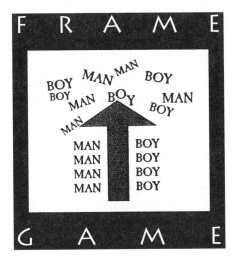

90.

The houses on a street are numbered 1, 2, 3, 4, 5, etc., up one side of the street; then the numbers continue consecutively on the other side of the street and work their way back to be opposite number 1. If house number 12 is opposite house number 29, how many houses are there on both sides of the street?

🪛 91.

Maria covered the first half of a bicycle race at 20 miles per hour. The second half of the race was a return over the same route, and her return speed was 30 miles per hour. What was Maria's average speed for the entire trip? Take your time with this.

🪛 92.

One of the five following figures does not belong with the rest. Which one is it, and why?

A   B   C   D   E

🪛 93.

A boat is coming downstream at 30 mph. On its return, it travels at 10 mph. The trip downstream is three hours shorter than the trip upstream. How far is it from the beginning of the trip to the turnaround point downstream?

🪛 94.

If Alicia is three times as old as Amy will be when Alex is as old as Alicia is now, who is the second oldest? Can you give their ages now?

95.

What 12-letter word is written in the block below? Start with any letter and move one letter at a time, in any direction, but don't go back over any letter!

O   I   R   T

G   N   E   T

O   M   R   Y

 96.

Fill in the two missing numbers in the following boxes.

Hint: Think outside the boxes.

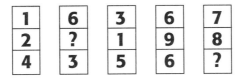

1	6	3	6	7
2	?	1	9	8
4	3	5	6	?

 97.

A certain pipe can fill a swimming pool in two hours; another pipe can fill it in five hours; a third pipe can empty the pool in six hours. With all three pipes turned on exactly at the same time, and starting with an empty pool, how long will it take to fill the pool?

 98.

Can you find 50 different words in the word "arithmetic"?

99.

Given the initial letters of the missing words, complete this sentence.

There are 5 S to a P.

 100.

Find the hidden phrase or title.

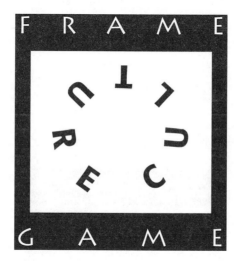

 101.

The proportion of southpaws among pitchers is greater than among players in general. Is there a statement that can be made for certain about the proportion of pitchers among left-handers compared to all ballplayers? Is it greater, smaller, or the same, or is there not enough information to tell?

Can you discover what is going on in the following figures? What is the relationship among the circles, squares, and dividing line that determines the respective numbers? What number goes with the sixth figure?

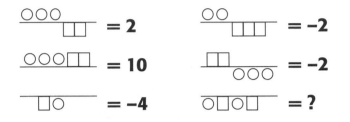

$$\frac{OOO}{\square\square} = 2 \qquad \frac{OO}{\square\square\square} = -2$$

$$\frac{OOO\square\square}{} = 10 \qquad \frac{\square\square}{OOO} = -2$$

$$\frac{}{\square O} = -4 \qquad \frac{O\square O\square}{} = \, ?$$

102.

103.

Find the hidden phrase or title.

FRAME

LINESTANDING

GAME

104.

What is the next number in this sequence?

5   6   8   7   9   3   4   5   10   2   11   ?

105.

Draw a square. Now divide the square into four equal, congruent parts with three straight lines. None of the lines may cross each other within the square.

106.

Find the hidden phrase or title.

107.

Change the position of one match stick to correct the following equation.

Hint: Think Roman.

 108.

Quickly now, which of the following symbols denotes mercury in the periodic table of the elements?

Me Mr Hg Hr My

 109.

At a reception, one-third of the guests departed at a certain time. Later, two-fifths of the remaining guests departed. Even later, two-thirds of those guests departed. If six people were left, how many were originally at the party?

 110.

Here is a word that needs to be unscrambled into an ordinary word recognizable to most anyone:

CRICKARFREE

111.

Find the hidden phrase or title.

 112.

Move from the first word to the last in six moves,
changing one letter each time to form a new word.

TREAT

———
———
———
———
———

BLOND

The dreaded cube-eaters from the fourth dimension descend upon a stack of 27 identical sugar cubes. Cube-eaters can only eat to the center of a cube. When they reach the center, they always make a 90° turn and proceed to the next cube. They never reenter a cube. If a cube-eater enters at location A, what is the minimum number of cubes it will eat through to reach the cube at location B?

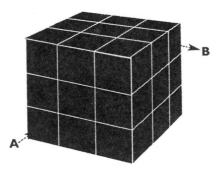

114.

What are the next two numbers in the following sequence, and why? (Consider only the first nine numbers.)

8 5 4 9 1 7 6 ? ?

115.

How many individual cubes are in this stack of cubes? Assume that all rows and columns are complete unless you actually see them end.

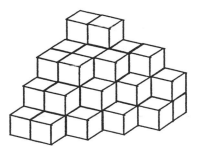

 116.

Find the hidden phrase or title.

117.

Five types of flowers grow in five gardens on five different streets. Given the following information, determine which flowers grow where.

1. The Smiths do not grow violets.
2. The Morgans grow peonies; they do not live on 2nd Street.
3. The Parks live on 3rd Street.
4. Begonias bloom on 4th Street.
5. Roses do not grow on 5th Street.
6. The Johnsons do not live on 1st Street.
7. The Rosens do not grow daffodils.
8. The Johnsons grow roses.
9. Daffodils grow on 1st Street.

118.

What is the missing number in this sequence?

$$(7, 8) \quad (19, 27) \quad (37, 64) \quad (61, 125)$$
$$(91, 216) \quad (\underline{?}, 343)$$

119.

You have the four kings and four queens from a deck of cards. Place the queens on top of the kings face-down in one stack. Pick up the stack, and starting with the top card (queen), place it faceup on a table. Take the second card and place it facedown on the bottom of the cards in your hand; place the third card faceup on the table, the fourth card on the bottom, and so on, until all cards are faceup. What is the order of the cards that are faceup?

120.

Find the hidden phrase or title.

121.

Given the initial letters of the missing words, complete this sentence.

There are 14 D in a F.

122.

See if you can unscramble the following words to make a sensible sentence out of them.

Last they say who best laughs or, he laughs so.

123.

Here's another "trickle-down" puzzle. Change one letter on each line to reach the final word. There may be more than one way to do this puzzle.

P E S T

    —————

    —————

    —————

B A T S

124.

Find the hidden phrase or title.

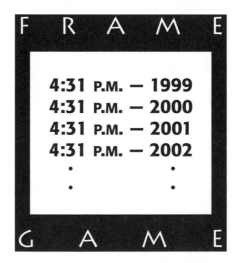

125.

Below are three intersecting circles that have a maximum of seven bounded areas that are not further subdivided. What is the maximum number of bounded areas that result when six circles are intersected?

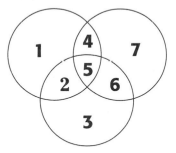

126.

Here is a form of syllogism. Assume that the first three statements are true and then determine whether the fourth statement, the conclusion, is valid or false. That's all there is to it!

Some *zers* are *tifs*.
All *tifs* are *xorts*.
Some *xorts* are *wols*.
Therefore, some *zers* are definitely *wols*.

127.

There is an old puzzle that asks you to come up with the longest word you can create using only the letter keys from the top row of a typewriter. Those letters are: Q, W, E, R, T, Y, U, I, O, and P. The solution to that puzzle is the 10-letter word TYPEWRITER.

Here's a new twist. Can you make at least one nine-letter word from those same letters? You may use any of the letters more than once.

128.

Find the hidden phrase or title.

 129.

If 14 equals 12 and 34 equals 38, what does 24 equal?

 130.

What follows is an argument: a premise and a conclusion based on that premise. See if you can determine whether the argument is valid or invalid.

> If we are to survive and prosper as a species, solving the riddles of the universe via mathematics becomes the single most important focus of theoreticians. Thus, only the most brilliant minds will succeed.

131.

Unscramble these letters to make a word:

R A L L E A P L

 132.

One glass is one-sixth full of blue liquid dye. Another glass, exactly the same size, is one-seventh full of the blue dye. Each glass is then filled to the top with water and their contents mixed together in a large container. What proportion of this final mixture is blue dye and what proportion is water?

 133.

Find the hidden phrase or title.

134.

One of the figures shown here lacks a characteristic common to the other five. Which figure is it, and why?

Hint: Don't consider symmetry.

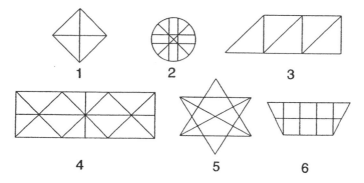

1   2   3

4   5   6

135.

Find the hidden phrase or title.

136.

A ten-letter word is hidden here. The last letter, R, is placed outside the grid of the other letters. Using each letter only once, and beginning with the first letter of the word, which may be in any of the nine positions of the grid, spell the word by moving up, down, sideways, or diagonally to adjacent letters.

```
        A    L    C
   R    O    C    U
        T    A    L
```

 137.

Find the hidden phrase or title.

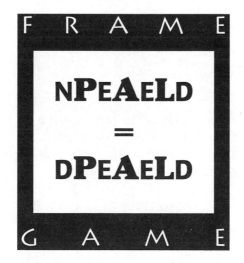

138.

In the following puzzle, the first number in each box has a certain relationship with the second number in that box. The relationships are the same for all four boxes. What is the missing number?

1	0		3	26		12	1,727		−2	?

 139.

This next sequence puzzle is math related, but not exactly what you might think at first. Fill in the missing term.

Hint 1: Think leap year.

Hint 2: Be careful! Some calculators will give you the wrong answer.

$$0-3-4-4-8-2-\underline{}$$

 140.

Here's a somewhat different perspective on the counting of stacked cubes. How many total cubes are there? Assume that all rows and columns are complete unless you actually see them end.

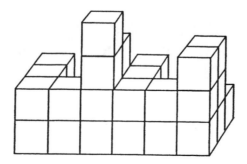

141.

Four married couples live on a street in four different-colored houses. Given the information below, can you determine who is married to whom and the color of their house? (One of the houses is red.)

    1. Harry does not live in the white house.
    2. Alice is not married to Brad.
    3. Steve lives in the yellow house.
    4. John is not married to June.
    5. Harry does not live in the blue house.
    6. Alice lives in the blue house.
    7. June is married to Harry.
    8. Nancy is not married to Steve.
    9. Sara is one of the wives.

142.

Find the hidden phrase or title.

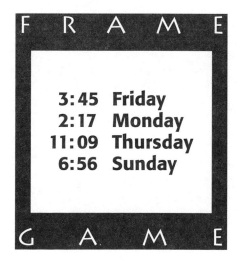

143.

Given the following letters and numbers, come up with the correct phrase:

There are 24 k in p g.

 144.

All the words listed below share a common theme. What is it?

> **Timer**
> **Spool**
> **Reward**
> **Emit**
> **Diaper**
> **Desserts**

 145.

See if you can ascertain the nature of the relationship among the pictures in each row in order to fill in the missing figure in row 3.

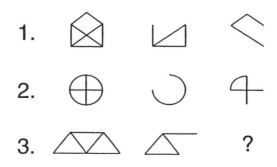

146.

Find the hidden phrase or title.

147.

I am six times as old as my sister. In one year I will be five times as old as my sister will be. In six years I will be three times as old as my sister will be. How old am I and how old is my sister?

148.

The three words on the left have an interesting characteristic that is reversed with the three words on the right. Can you identify what that characteristic (and its reverse) is?

federal	defy
pond	hijack
ruts	calmness

149.

Sometimes people wonder whether puzzles have any real-life applications. You be the judge. Here's an example:

A mother was throwing a birthday party for her daughter and realized that, with only nine scoops of ice cream, there wasn't enough to give two scoops to each of the five children present. She quickly came up with an idea that pleased all—and everyone got an equal amount of ice cream. By the way, she did not divide the scoops into fractional portions. How did this real-life mom solve her dilemma?

150.

Here is an *alphametic* (alphabet arithmetic problem): Fred, a football fanatic, is going to his first University of Nebraska football game. He doesn't know that Nebraska has the nation's longest streak of consecutive sellouts for their home games. See if you can find the number of people that were sitting in the north end zone with Fred. Each letter in the following alphametic retains the same value within the problem, and the value must be different from that of any other letter. Zero may not begin a word.

$$
\begin{array}{r}
\text{RED} \\
\text{RED} \\
\text{RED} \\
\text{FRED} \\
\hline
\text{HORDE}
\end{array}
$$

151.

Find the hidden phrase or title.

152.

Here are five words. The first four are newly created English words that are related to their respective patterns. For the fifth pattern, you have to come up with the word; for the last word, you have to come up with the pattern.

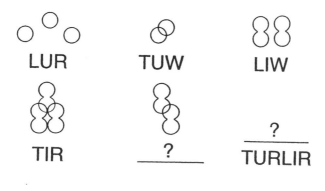

LUR TUW LIW

TIR ? TURLIR

153.

You are playing a game with a friend called "penny pickup" in which nine pennies are placed on a table. In alternating turns, each player picks up at least one, but not more than five pennies per turn. The player who picks up the last penny wins. However, the penny has to be by itself for that player to win. In other words, if your opponent picks up five pennies, you can't pick up four and call yourself the winner. Under these guidelines, if you go first, is there a move you can make to ensure that you win?

 154.

Find the hidden phrase or title.

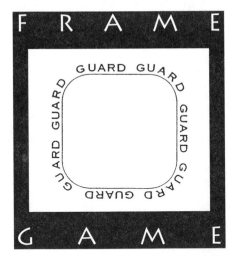

155.

At a convention of baseball trading card collectors, 30 dealers are interested in trading or selling their extra Mickey Mantle cards. Fifteen of the dealers have fewer than five such cards to trade, 11 others have more than six of them to trade, and three others have more than seven to trade or sell. What is the total number of dealers that have five, six, or seven Mickey Mantle cards?

156.

Here is a series challenge for the better brainteaser fan. Fill in the missing term in this mathematical series.

$$9-73-241-561-1{,}081-1{,}849-?$$

 157.

A zookeeper has to put 27 snakes in four cages. His problem is that he must have an odd number of snakes in each cage. How can he accomplish this? You can put any number of snakes in a cage as long as the total number of snakes in each cage is an odd number.

158.

Given the following letters and numbers, come up with the correct phrase.

   Hint: This is not a particularly common phrase, but it's soluble. Think "game."

225S on a SB

159.

Find the hidden phrase or title.

160.

What is the next letter in the following odd sequence?

$$O-T-F-S-N-E-\underline{\quad}$$

161.

Bob was paddling his canoe upstream at a constant rate. After six miles, the wind blew his hat into the stream. Thinking that he had no chance to recover his hat, he continued upstream for six more miles before turning back. He continued rowing at the same rate on his return trip and overtook his hat at exactly the same spot where he began his journey, eight hours earlier. What was the velocity of the stream?

162.

What is the fewest number of lines that would need to be erased to do away with all of the triangles in this figure?

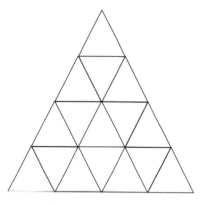

 163.

In five minutes, how many words can you make out of the word ***crazed*** (any number of letters allowed)?

 164.

A traveler at an airport had lots of time to kill between flights, so he decided to conduct an experiment on one of the moving walkways. He found he could walk the length of the walkway, moving in its forward direction, in one minute. Walking at the same rate *against* the forward direction of the walkway, it took him three minutes to cover the same distance. He wondered how long it would take him to cover one length if the walkway were to stop. Can you help him out? (This may not be as easy as it first appears.)

165.

Find the hidden phrase or title.

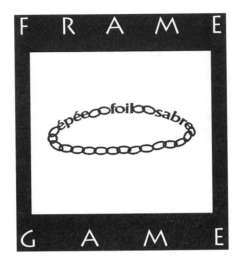

166.

What letter comes next in the following sequence?
Hint: Go straight to the answer.

$$A-E-F-H-I-K-L-M-N-\underline{\quad}$$

167

Which one of the following patterns does not belong with the rest?

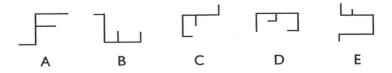

A   B   C   D   E

168.

Using three nines, what is the largest number that can be created? You may use any mathematical symbols or signs you wish, with the exception of infinity (∞) and ellipses (...). You may not use the three nines together in combination, such as 99 × 9. In other words, each nine must remain by itself before any math operation is performed on it. Additionally, no mathematical symbol or sign may be used more than four times.

 169.

Unscramble the following:

CITURSIUFT

 170.

Find the hidden phrase or title.

171.

A box of candy can be divided equally among three, five, or thirteen people. What is the smallest number of pieces of candy the box can contain?

172.

What 9-letter word is written in the block below? Start with any letter and move one letter at a time, in any direction, but don't go back over any letter!

O N N
C U D
M U R

173.

What is the missing number in the following series?
Hint: Tackling this puzzle head-on won't help you. Try different directions.

23—48—9—39—___—51—12—37

174.

The six words listed here share a common trait. What is it?

pride—slime—grant—price—globe—whole

175.

Try your luck at this "trickle-down" puzzle. Remember, change one letter at a time to arrive at the answer.

P U L L
_____
_____
_____
B I T E

 176.

Unscramble these letters to make a word.

YONNMSY

 177.

Here is a list of scores from a fictitious college football season. Based on the given scores only, see if you can figure out who would win and by how much if Harvard were to play Montana during this season.

Montana 27   **Notre Dame 13**
Harvard 17   **New Hampshire 16**
Notre Dame 14   **Ohio State 10**
New Hampshire 24   **Connecticut 21**
Ohio State 10   **BYU 7**
Connecticut 28   **Maine 24**
Maine 35   **BYU 3**

178.

Find the hidden phrase or title.

179.

The following is in code. Can you crack the code and decipher the message?

JZF'CP LD JZFYR LD JZF QPPW

ANSWERS

1. Pete has $^8/_{35}$ of the candy. Here's how to get the answer: After Joe takes $^3/_5$ of the candy, $^2/_5$ of the bag is left. If we let Pete's share be x and Bob's share be $^3/_4x$, we have

$$x + {}^3/_4x = {}^2/_5$$
$${}^7/_4x = {}^2/_5$$
$$x = {}^2/_5 \times {}^4/_7$$
$$x = {}^8/_{35}$$

Thus, Pete has $^8/_{35}$ of the candy and Bob has $^6/_{35}$ of the candy.

2. F = 23. Substituting Eq. (1) in Eq. (2), gives

$$A + B + P = T$$

And substituting Eq. (5) in this last equation gives

$$8 + B + P = T \qquad (6)$$

If we then substitute Eq. (3) in Eq. (4), we get

$$B + P + T + A = 30$$

Substituting Eq. (5) in this last equation gives

$$22 - B - P = T \qquad (7)$$

Adding Eqs. (6) and (7) gives the following:

$$8 + B + P = T$$
$$\underline{22 - B - P = T}$$
$$30 = 2T$$
$$\text{So, T} = 15 \qquad (8)$$

Substituting Eqs. (5) and (8) in Eq. (3) gives

$$F = 15 + 8 = 23$$

3. Ser

4. The order should be 4, 1, 3, 5, 2.

5. One possible answer:

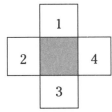

6.   1) CAGI

        2)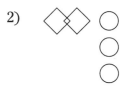

The breakdown of the relationships:

        D = Horizontal

        C = Vertical

        A = ◯

        E = ◇

        G = 3

        B = 2

        Y = Uncoupled

        I = Coupled

7. 168. The pattern behind this sequence can be revealed by factoring the individual terms:

$$5 = 2^2 + 1$$
$$8 = 3^2 - 1$$
$$26 = 5^2 + 1$$
$$48 = 7^2 - 1$$
$$122 = 11^2 + 1$$

This shows that the squares of the prime numbers are involved. So the next term in the sequence must be

$$13^2 = 168$$
$$169 - 1 = 168$$

8. Getting it all together

9. Bleary. Take the last three letters of each pair of words to form the new words.

10. MCDXLIX

11. It should be placed 16 ft to the right of the fulcrum.

Left side: Currently there is a total of
20 ft × 40 lb + 10 ft × 20 lb = 800 + 200 = 1,000 ft lb

Right side: Currently there is 10 ft × 60 lb = 600 ft lb. Since this is less than what's on the left side, the 25-lb weight must go somewhere on the right side. Let's call the exact distance from the fulcrum y:

$$10 \times 60 + 25y = 1,000$$
$$25y = 400$$
$$y = 400/25 = 16 \text{ ft}$$

12. A bad spell of flu

13. $1\frac{1}{2}$

14. 21%. If you were to pick a student at random, the probability that he or she was taking at least one of the courses is 64% + 22% − 7% = 79%, which means there is a 21% chance that the student was taking neither course.

15. A = 1, B = 3, C = 2. We can arrive at the answer via a plan of attack that examines the rules one at a time to chart the possibilities:

Rule (a): This tells us too little at this point.

Rule (b): This raises two clear possibilities:

B = 2, A = 3, C = 1
or
B = 1, A = 3, C = 2

Let's assume one of these is correct and look at the next two rules.

Rule (c): This eliminates possibility (1).

Rule (d): This eliminates possibility (2). But what if C = 3 while B = 1 or 2? That raises the following two possibilities:

B = 2, A = 1, C = 3
or
B = 1, A = 2, C = 3

Rule (e): This eliminates possibilities (3) and (4). Thus, B is not 1 or 2 and so it must be 3.

Rule (f): If B = 3, then A, not being 2, must be 1. And C, therefore, must be 2.

16. Here's one way:

TIMER
TIMES
DIMES
DINES
DUNES
DUNKS

17. "All Things Great and Small"

18. There are six outs in an inning.

19. The glass is $5/16$ empty. The $5/8$ is equal to $10/16$, which means that if the glass were $10/16$ full, you would have emptied $6/16$ of it. You empty $5/16$ of the glass first.

20. 125. 5 is 25 times $1/5$; likewise, 125 is 25 times 5.

21. British Open

22. D. Beginning with the S at the top of the first triangle and moving counterclockwise, the letters spell out STRETCH YOUR MIND.

23. Check-kiting

24. Eleven. Tom had to win four matches to draw even with Bill, and then Tom had to win three more times:

$$4 + 4 + 3 = 11$$

25. She is their aunt.

26. Ants in his pants

27. Here's one way to solve this:

$$^{8888}/_{88} = 101; 101 - {}^{8}/_{8} = 100$$

28. Here are three. Can you find more?

aardvark

mascara

anagram

29. "Star Wars"

30. 151. In each column, divide the top number by 3 to get the bottom number. Then add 3 to the sum of the top and bottom numbers to get the middle number.

31. Zero. The fisherman caught 3, 6, 9, and 12 fish on the second, third, fourth, and fifth days, respectively. If we let x represent the number of fish caught on the first day, then

$$x + (x + 3) + (x + 6) + (x + 9) + (x + 12) = 30$$
$$x + x + 3 + x + 6 + x + 9 + x + 12 = 30$$
$$5x + 30 = 30$$
$$5x = 0$$
$$x = 0$$

32. 86,400 seconds in a day

33. SCRABBLE

34. 24

35. 321. Divide 3 into 960 and add 1 (for the first term in the sequence).

36.

$$\begin{array}{r} 15 \\ \times 35 \\ \hline 75 \\ 45 \\ \hline 525 \end{array}$$

37. Pace back and forth.

38. The amateur's mother

39.

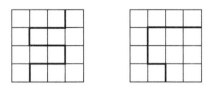

40. Because your chances of winning are 1 in 9. The probability of rolling a 2 is $^1/_{36}$; of a 3 is $^2/_{36}$; and of a 12 is $^1/_{36}$. And $^1/_{36} + ^2/_{36} + ^1/_{36} = ^4/_{36} = ^1/_9$. Thank your friend and buy him a drink.

41. 52%. First, we express the given fractions in terms of the least common denominator. Thus,

$$^1/_7 = {}^{11}/_{77} \text{ and } ^3/_{11} = {}^{21}/_{77}$$

Now we can restate the question as

"$^{11}/_{77}$ is what percent of $^{21}/_{77}$?"

This is the same as "11 is what percent of 21?"
And $^{11}/_{21} = 52\%$ (approximately).

42. Tocopherol is vitamin E. All the rest are minerals.

43. Reverse the charges.

44. $\dfrac{1}{2\sqrt{3}}$ or $\dfrac{\sqrt{3}}{6}$

Let the original fraction be $\dfrac{1}{x}$:

$$\frac{1}{x} \times \frac{4}{5} \times \frac{1}{x} = \frac{4}{5x^2}$$

$$\frac{4}{5x^2} = \frac{1}{15}$$

$$5x^2 = 60$$

$$x^2 = 12$$

$$x = \sqrt{12}$$

$$x = \sqrt{4 \times 3}$$

$$x = 2\sqrt{3}$$

$$\text{Ans. } = \frac{1}{2\sqrt{3}} \quad \text{or} \quad \frac{\sqrt{3}}{6}$$

45.

$$26^2 = 676$$
$$101^2 = 10{,}201$$

73

46. Let x = number of $0.50 candles, y = the number of $5.50 candles, and z = the number of $9.50 candles. From the problem statement we know that

$$x + y + z = 100 \qquad (1)$$
$$0.50x + 5.50y + 9.50z = 100 \qquad (2)$$

We can now multiply Eq. (1) by –0.5 and add it to Eq. (2):

$$-0.5x - 0.5y - 0.5z = -50$$
$$+0.5x + 5.5y + 9.5z = +100$$

Thus,

$$5y = 50 - 9z$$
$$y = 10 - \frac{9}{5}z$$

Since we're dealing with whole numbers, z must be a whole number and a multiple of 5. In this case, z can equal only 5, because with any greater number y would become negative. So

$z = 5$, $y = 1$ and thus x must be 94 candles at $.50 each.

47. 30. Triangles ABC, ABE, ABH, ABI, ACD, ACE, ACH, ADH, AEF, AFG, AFH, AGH, AHI, BCD, BCH, BCI, BDH, BEH, BGH, CEF, CEH, CEJ, CFH, CFJ, CHI, DGH, EFH, EHJ, FHI, and FHJ

48. The odd one out

49. J. These are the first letters of the months of the year, starting with December and running backward.

50. $A = 1$ $B = 8$ $C = 9$
 $D = 3$ $E = 4$ $F = 6$
 Thus, $1 \times 8 \times 9 = 72 = 3 \times 4 \times 6$.

51. Here's one. Can you find others?

post
spot
tops
pots
opts

52. 30 beasts and 15 birds. Let b be the number of beasts and B be the number of birds. From the total number of feet, we know that

$$B(2 \text{ feet/bird}) + b(4 \text{ feet/beast}) = 150, \text{ or}$$
$$2B + 4b = 150$$

The total number of creatures is $B + b = 45$,
$$\text{so } B = 45 - b$$

Now we can substitute this last equation into the feet equation:

$$2(45 - b) + 4b = 150$$
$$90 - 2b + 4b = 150$$
$$2b = 60$$
$$b = 30 \text{ beasts and } B = 45 - 30 = 15 \text{ birds}$$

53. $^1/_3$. The relationship between successive numbers, beginning with the first 240, is:

$$1, {}^1/_2, {}^1/_3, {}^1/_4, {}^1/_5 \text{ and } {}^1/_6.$$
$$^1/_6 \times 2 = {}^1/_3$$

54. 50. Compare the two equations as presented in this diagram:

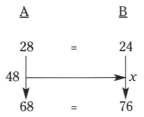

As you can see from the diagram, 48 is the midpoint between 28 and 68. We now need to find the midpoint between 24 and 76. We do this by adding 24 and 76, which equals 100, and dividing that by 2. Therefore, the answer is 50.

55. The word is PUZZLES. The answer can be obtained by putting each letter of the alphabet in a 5 x 5 grid, with *Y* and *Z* sharing the last box. The two-digit numbers are decoded by making the row number the tens digit and the column number the units digit of the letter being sought. Thus, for example, the code 41 represents row 4, column 1, which is the letter P. (*Note:* It was the ancient Greek historian Polybius who first proposed a similar method of substituting numbers for letters.)

	1	2	3	4	5
1	A	B	C	D	E
2	F	G	H	I	J
3	K	L	M	N	O
4	P	Q	R	S	T
5	U	V	W	X	Y/Z

56. 90º

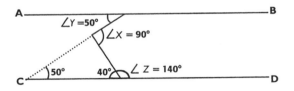

57. The figures correspond to each other as follows: A to E, B to F, C to G, and D to H. Blank squares in Figures A through D are filled with Xs in corresponding Figures E through H. Filled squares in Figures A through D are made blank. The correct figure is shown below.

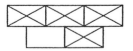

58. Each of the words can be made into at least two other words:

rifle: flier, lifer
evil: live, vile (and veil)
deal: lead, dale
rats: star, arts (and tars)
tale: late, teal

59. Only one doctor is a dermatologist. The other 99 are, of course, surgeons.

60. 76 trombones in the big parade

61. B

62. $93.26

$$
\begin{array}{r}
2442 \\
5442 \\
\underline{1442} \\
93.26
\end{array}
$$

63. There are fifty-four external sides (the number of faces on nine cubes). Since two gallons are needed to paint one cube, you would need 2 x 9, or 18 gallons of paint to cover the figure.

64. 1. The first nine numbers of this sequence will repeat to infinity when the consecutive integers from 1 to 9 are squared and the resultant digits added together until a one-digit number is achieved:

$$1^2 = 1$$
$$2^2 = 4$$
$$3^2 = 9$$
$$4^2 = 16, \text{ and } 1 + 6 = 7$$
$$5^2 = 25, \text{ and } 2 + 5 = 7$$
$$6^2 = 36, \text{ and } 3 + 6 = 9$$
$$7^2 = 49, \text{ and } 4 + 9 = 13 \text{ and } 1 + 3 = 4$$
$$8^2 = 64, \text{ and } 6 + 4 = 10 \text{ and } 1 + 0 = 1$$
$$9^2 = 81, \text{ and } 8 + 1 = 9$$
$$10^2 = 100, \text{ and } 1 + 0 = 1$$

65. Line up in single file.

66. The value of R is 20. Because it is known that Q + M = C, it follows that Q + M + K = R. We also know that R + Q = S, so in the equation M + K + S = 40, we can replace S with R + Q. The equation then becomes M + K + R + Q = 40, or M + K + R = 32 because Q is 8. Rearranging the equations to solve for R, we then have:

$$8 + M + K = R$$
$$32 - M - K = R$$

$$40 = 2R \text{ and therefore R } 20$$
$$\text{Because R + Q = S}$$
$$20 + 8 = S$$
$$S = 28$$

67. Tomorrow is another day.

68. $$\frac{4!}{\sqrt{4}} = \frac{4 \times 3 \times 2 \times 1}{2} = 12$$

69. The missing number is 259. Starting with 1, the sequence is follows:

$$1^2, 2^2 + 1, 3^2 + 2, 4^2 + 3 \text{ (first circle)}$$
$$1^3, 2^3 + 1, 3^3 + 2, 4^3 + 3 \text{ (second circle)}$$
$$1^4, 2^4 + 1, 3^4 + 2, 4^4 + 3 \text{ (third circle)}$$

70. Crime wave

71.

$$\underline{\mathbf{1 T \Gamma}}$$

These are the numbers 1, 3, 5, 7, 9, and 11, back to back with their reverse images.

72. $1/2$ lb. The $1/5$ lb of chocolate is equivalent to $2/5$ of a block of chocolate. Multiply the $1/5$ lb by $5/2$ to find the weight of the whole block:

$$1/5 \times 5/2 = 5/10 = 1/2 \text{ lb}$$

73. Fight breaking out (or fighting across the border)

74. His wife bets the opposite of whatever her husband bets, usually double or triple the amount that he has placed.

75.

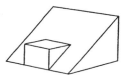

76. $\dfrac{2}{1}$.

These are the ratios of the frequencies of the eight notes of the diatonic scale, beginning with C. They are usually written

$$\frac{1}{1} : \frac{9}{8} : \frac{5}{4} : \frac{4}{3} : \text{etc.}$$

77. A piece of the pie

78. LATITUDE

79. 5:00 A.M.

80. D

81. BAR

82. You bet it makes a difference! If $\frac{1}{30}$ were the true mean of $\frac{1}{40}$ and $\frac{1}{20}$, then neither dealer would have an advantage. However, the mean of $\frac{1}{40}$ and $\frac{1}{20}$ is 0.0375. The fraction $\frac{1}{30}$ is equivalent to 0.0333! So the buyers at the store across the street are being taken to the cleaners. The average of the reciprocals of two numbers is not the same as the reciprocal of the average.

83. There's a fine line between love and hate.

84. If you had three quarters, four dimes, and four pennies, which totals $1.19, you couldn't make change for a dollar.

85. Name

86. No room for error

87. In 15 years. There are several ways to solve this puzzle, one of which uses a chart comparing their movements. It helps to realize that the correct answer must involve whole-number (not fractional) revolutions.

y (3 years)	x (5 years)
3 years = 1 revolution	$3/5$ revolution
6 years = 2 revolutions	$1^1/_5$ revolutions
9 years = 3 revolutions	$1^4/_5$ revolutions
12 years = 4 revolutions	$2^2/_5$ revolutions
15 years = 5 revolutions	3 revolutions

88. 7, 0. If you take the difference between each of the numbers, respecting whether that difference is positive or negative, you will find the following pattern:

$$3, 3, -7, 3, 3, -7, 3 \ldots$$

As you can see from this pattern, the next difference needs to be 3, which makes the first answer 7. The next difference is –7, which makes the second answer 0.

89. Separating the men from the boys

90. 40. Here's one way to figure this out: there are 16 houses between number 12 and number 29. Since half of those have to be on each side, there are 8 more houses on each side. This makes the last home on one side house number 20, and there must be 20 more homes going back up the street, which makes a total of 40.

91. 24 miles per hour. Let's say Maria went 60 miles up and 60 miles back. It would then take her three hours up and two hours to get back. Five hours to go 120 miles is $^{120}/_5 =$ 24 miles per hour.

92. C. This is the only figure that has both concave and convex features. The other figures have one or the other only.

93. 45 miles. Let x be the distance from the beginning point to the turnaround point, and let y be the time it takes to go downstream. Then

Downstream: $\dfrac{x \text{ mi}}{30 \text{ mph}} = y$ (1)

Upstream: $\dfrac{x \text{ mi}}{10 \text{ mph}} = y + 3$

$$\dfrac{x}{10} - 3 = y \qquad (2)$$

Setting Eq. (1) equal to Eq. (2) gives

$$\dfrac{x}{30} = \dfrac{x}{10} - 3$$

$$x = 3x - 90$$

$$2x = 90$$

$$x = 45 \text{ miles}$$

94. Alex is the second oldest. Their ages are:

      Alicia: 30 years old
      Alex: 25 years old
      Amy: 5 years old

95. TRIGONOMETRY

96. 7 in the second column, and 5 in the last column. If you delete the boxes and move the numbers together, you have a simple addition problem:

$$\begin{array}{r} 16367 \\ +27198 \\ \hline 43565 \end{array}$$

97. $1\frac{7}{8}$ hours. In one hour, the first pipe fills half the pool, the second pipe fills $\frac{1}{5}$, and the third pipe empties $\frac{1}{6}$. That is, in one hour the pool fills:

$$\frac{1}{2} + \frac{1}{5} - \frac{1}{6} = \frac{15}{30} + \frac{6}{30} - \frac{5}{30}$$
$$= \frac{16}{30}$$
$$= \frac{8}{15}$$

For the whole pool to fill, then, it takes $\frac{15}{8} = 1\frac{7}{8}$ hours.

98. Here are the ones we found. Did you find others?

math	thrice	timer	heat
rich	rice	crime	eat
chime	mice	crate	cheat
chimera	metric	cream	came
rat	time	ream	tame
cat	rime	treat	hater
hat	cite	threat	rate
mat	rite	tire	ate
tic	hate	mire	tea
mirth	mate	hire	team
chair	matte	it	mart
hair	act	teach	art
mare	tact	reach	cart
hare	them	meat	heart

99. There are five sides to a pentagon.

100. Counterculture revolution

101. Greater. Let x be the number of southpaws that are pitchers, y be the number of all southpaws, p be the number of all pitchers, and q be the number of all ballplayers. Then we have

$$\frac{x}{p} > \frac{y}{q} \text{ or } xq > yp \text{ or } \frac{x}{y} > \frac{p}{q}$$

102. −8. Above the line, either figure, circle or square, is worth +2 points apiece. Below the line, either figure is worth −2 points apiece. It makes no difference whether it is the circle or the square that comes first.

103. Standing at the end of the line

104. 6. Starting at the left, each group of three numbers adds up to 19.

105. Here is one way:

106. Root canal

107. Remove the vertical match in the plus sign and place it next to the match sticks at the beginning of the equation

$$(3 - 1 = 2)$$

108. Hg

109. 45. When $\frac{1}{3}$ left, $\frac{2}{3}$ of the people remained. When $\frac{2}{5}$ left, $\frac{3}{5}$ of $\frac{2}{3}$ remained. When $\frac{2}{3}$ of the remaining people left, $\frac{3}{5}$ of $\frac{2}{3}$ of $\frac{1}{3}$ (or $\frac{6}{45}$) of the people remained. Since there were 6 people remaining, there were originally 45 people.

110. FIRECRACKER

111. Tailgate party

112. Here's one way:
TREAT
TREAD
BREAD
BREED
BLEED
BLEND
BLOND

113. Seven

114. 3 and then 2. The numbers are arranged in the alphabetical order of their spelled-out names.

115. 44

116. It's hip to be square.

117.

Daffodils	Smiths	1st Street
Roses	Johnsons	2nd Street
Violets	Parks	3rd Street
Begonias	Rosens	4th Street
Peonies	Morgans	5th Street

118. The missing number is 127. Starting with (7, 8), the difference between each enclosed pair of numbers is: 1^3, 2^3, 3^3, 4^3, 5^3, 6^3.

$$6^3 = 216$$
$$343 - 216 = 127$$

119. Queen, queen, king, king, queen, king, queen, king

120. Male bonding

121. There are 14 days in a fortnight.

122. He who laughs last laughs best, or so they say.

123. Here's one solution:

PEST
PAST
PASS
BASS
BATS

124. Same time next year

125. There are 31 bounded areas that are not further subdivided. One way to approach this puzzle is to look for a pattern: two circles have three bounded areas; three circles have seven; four circles have 13. Five circles would then have 21 bounded areas. The pattern is increasing 4, 6, 8, 10, 12...so six circles would have 21 + 10 or 31 bounded areas.

126. False. Some *zers* <u>may be</u> *wols*, but there is nothing to support the conclusion that some *zers* are definitely *wols*.

127. Here's one: POTPOURRI. What are some others?

128. A star in the making

129. It equals 25. Compare the two equations in the question:

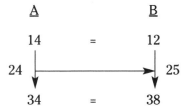

The midpoint of column A is 24; the midpoint of column B is 25.

130. False. Even if the premise were true, it does not automatically follow that only the most brilliant minds will succeed. The conclusion is too open-ended. Who determines what represents brilliance? Is it simply a matter of intelligence tests, or are there other considerations? Who chooses the criteria? Who decides what success is? Many questions need to be answered before this argument can be considered valid.

131. PARALLEL

132. 13:71

Glass 1 is $\frac{1}{6}$ dye $+\frac{5}{6}$ water

Glass 2 is $\frac{1}{7}$ dye $+\frac{6}{7}$ water

Total dye in mixture =

$$\frac{1}{6} + \frac{1}{7} = \frac{13}{42}$$

Total water in mixture =

$$\frac{5}{6} + \frac{6}{7} = \frac{35}{42} + \frac{36}{42} = \frac{71}{42}$$

$\frac{13}{42}$ parts blue dye and $\frac{71}{42}$ parts water

133. Open forum

134. Figure 5 is the only one that doesn't include a square in its design.

135. Piece of cake

136. CALCULATOR

137. A friend in need is a friend indeed.

138. –9. The second number in each box is 1 less than the cube of the first number.

139. 7. The decimal representation of the fraction $1/29$ is .0344827. On some calculators, the digit 7 in that number is rounded off to 8.

140. 35. Bottom level, 18; second level, 12; third level, 4; top level, 1.

141.

> Harry—June—Red
> John—Alice—Blue
> Brad—Nancy—White
> Steve—Sara—Yellow

142. A day at a time

143. There are 24 karats in pure gold.

144. Each is a different word when spelled backward. Such words are called recurrent palindromes.

145.

In each row, the pattern of lines in the second column has been subtracted from the pattern in the first column to produce the figure in the third column.

146. Meeting of the minds

147. I am 24 years old and my sister is 4 years old. Here's one way to derive the answer:

148. The words on the left have three consecutive letters of the alphabet in reverse order: <u>fed</u>eral, <u>pon</u>d, r<u>uts</u>. The words on the right have three consecutive letters of the alphabet in the correct order: <u>def</u>y, <u>hij</u>ack, cal<u>mn</u>ess.

149. She put all nine scoops of ice cream into a blender and made milk shakes.

150.

```
    982
    982
    982
  +7982
  ──────
 10,928
```

151. Spiral notebook

152. Here's how the words and the patterns are related: The letter L is used with the patterns whose individual components are separated. T goes with the patterns whose components are interlocked. R corresponds to three components and W to two. I goes with the snowman patterns, and U goes with the circles. For the two interlocked snowmen, the new word is TIW. The last pattern looks like this:

153. Pick up one penny on the first move and you can't be beat. Did you find any other winning move?

154. Border guards

155. Twelve. Since 15 dealers have fewer than 5 cards, those 15 are eliminated from consideration. Three have more than 7 cards, so they are eliminated. Eleven have more than 6 cards, which means all 11 must have exactly 7 cards. This totals to 15 + 3 + 11 = 29 dealers, leaving one dealer we haven't mentioned (tricky, huh?), who must have exactly 5 or 6 cards.

156. 2913. There are a couple of ways to solve this puzzle. The first way builds the series by summing squares and cubes in an interesting way:

$$1^2 + 2^3 = 1 + 8 = 9$$
$$3^2 + 4^3 = 9 + 64 = 73$$
$$5^2 + 6^3 = 25 + 168 = 241$$
$$7^2 + 8^3 = 49 + 512 = 561$$
$$9^2 + 10^3 = 81 + 1,000 = 1,081$$
$$11^2 + 12^3 = 121 + 1,728 = 1,849$$
$$13^2 + 14^3 = 169 + 2,744 = 2,913$$

Another approach involves taking the "difference of the differences." From the pattern continuing 48s that results, you can build back up the answer of 2913:

9		73		241		561		1,081		1,849		2,913
	64		168		320		520		768			1,064
		104		152		200		248				296
			48		48		48					48

157. Here's one way to solve the zookeeper's problem:

Put nine snakes in each of three cages, and put those three cages within a fourth, larger cage, in case any snakes escape from one of the smaller cages.

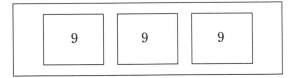

158. 225 squares on a Scrabble board

159. *The Rise and Fall of the Roman Empire*

160. T, for thirteen. These are the first letters of the odd numbers, in ascending order, beginning with one.

161. 1 mph. Bob was rowing at a constant rate in relation to the water, and it took him 8 hours to travel 24 miles. At the point where he lost his hat, he had been rowing for 6 miles, or 2 hours. To meet Bob where he began his journey, the hat had to travel downstream 6 miles. Bob didn't reach the hat until after he had rowed the remaining 18 miles, or for 6 more hours. Thus, it took the hat 6 hours to travel 6 miles, carried by the stream at a velocity of 1 mph.

$$6 \text{ miles}/6 \text{ hours} = 1 \text{ mph}$$

162. 4

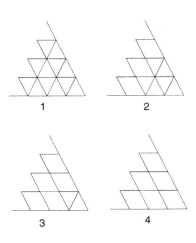

163. Here's a start:

raze	daze	red
race	read	dear
razed	dare	ace
raced	cared	aced
zed	care	are

164. 90 seconds. In 1 minute the man can walk 1 length in the forward direction, but only one-third of a length in the backward direction. Factoring out the effects of the walkway's speed, we find that in 1 minute the man can walk

$$\frac{1 + \frac{1}{3}}{2}$$

or $\frac{2}{3}$ of a length in one minute.

This means that the man can walk one length of the stationary walkway in $\frac{3}{2} \times 60 = 90$ seconds.

165. Chain link fencing

166. T. These are capital letters, beginning with A, that contain straight lines only.

167. C. All of the patterns contain a figure similar to a capital F except pattern C, which has a backwards F.

168. $(9!^{9!^{9!}})!$

169. FUTURISTIC

170. Placed under arrest

171. 195. The lowest common denominator of 3, 5, and 13 is $3 \times 5 \times 13 = 195$.

172. Conundrum

173. 21. Starting with the two outside numbers and moving toward the middle, each pair adds up to 60.

174. Each is a 5-letter word that becomes a 4-letter word when its first letter is removed.

175. Here's one version:

> PULL
> PILL
> PILE
> BILE
> BITE

176. SYNONYM

177. Harvard would beat Montana by 16 points. Here's how to find the answer:

Maine beat BYU by 32 – 3 = 29 points, and Ohio State beat BYU by 10 – 7 = 3 points.
So if Maine were to play Ohio State, they would win by 29 – 3 = 26 points.
Notre Dame beat Ohio State by 14 – 10 = 4 points and, since Maine would beat Ohio State by 26, they would beat Notre Dame by 26 – 4 = 22 points.
Montana beat Notre Dame by 27 – 13 = 14 points and, since Maine would beat Notre Dame by 22, they would beat Montana by 22 – 14 = 8 points.
But Connecticut beat Maine by 28 – 24 = 4 points, so, because Maine would beat Montana by 8, Connecticut would beat Montana by 4 + 8 = 12 points.
New Hampshire beat Connecticut by 24 – 21 = 3, so, because Connecticut would beat Montana by 12, New Hampshire would beat Montana by 3 + 12 + 15 points.
Finally, Harvard beat New Hampshire by 1 point, so, because New Hampshire would beat Montana by 15, Harvard would beat Montana by 1 + 15 = 16 points.

178. Lowering the boom

179. You're as young as you feel. To decode, find the code letter in the bottom row and translate it into the corresponding letter in the top row:

A B C D E F G H I J K L M N O P Q R S T U V W X Y Z
L M N O P Q R S T U V W X Y Z A B C D E F G H I J K

Index

Note: Answer page numbers are in italics.

WHAT IS AMERICAN MENSA?

AMERICAN MENSA
The High IQ Society

One out of 50 people qualifies
for American Mensa ...
Are YOU the One?

American Mensa, Ltd. is an organization for individuals who have one common trait: a score in the top two percent of the population on a standardized intelligence test. Over five million Americans are eligible for membership ... you may be one of them.

LOOKING FOR INTELLECTUAL STIMULATION?

You'll find a good "mental workout" in the Mensa Bulletin, our national magazine. Voice your opinion in the newsletter published by your local group. And attend activities and gatherings with fascinating programs and engaging conversation.

LOOKING FOR SOCIAL INTERACTION?

There's something happening on the Mensa calendar almost daily. These range from lectures to game nights to parties. Each year, there are over 40 regional gatherings and the Annual Gathering, where you can meet people, exchange ideas, and make interesting new friends.

LOOKING FOR OTHERS
WHO SHARE YOUR SPECIAL INTEREST?

Whether your interest might be computer gaming, the meaning of life, science fiction & fantasy, or scuba diving, there's probably a Mensa Special Interest Group (SIG) for you. There are over 150 SIGs, maintained by members just in the United States.

So visit our Web site for more information about American Mensa Ltd.

http://www.us.mensa.org

Or call our automated messaging system to request an application or for additional information:

(800) 66-MENSA

Or write to us at:

American Mensa Ltd.
1229 Corporate Drive West
Arlington, TX 76006

AmericanMensa@mensa.org

If you don't live in the United States and would like to get in touch with your national Mensa organization, contact:

Mensa International
15 The Ivories
6–8 Northampton Street, Islington
London N1 2HY England

www.mensa.org